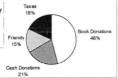

Arlington National Cemetery

Ted and Lola Schaefer

Heinemann Library
Chicago, Illinois

Designed by Richard Parker and Mike Hogg Design
Illustrations by Jeff Edwards
Originated by Chroma Graphics (Overseas) Pte Ltd.
Printed and bound in China by South China Printing Company

10 09 08 07 06
10 9 8 7 6 5 4 3 2 1

Library of Congress Cataloging-in-Publication Data
Schaefer, Ted, 1948-
  Arlington National Cemetery / Ted and Lola Schaefer.
    p. cm. -- (Symbols of freedom)
  Includes index.
  ISBN 1-4034-6665-3 (library binding (hardcover)) -- ISBN 1-4034-6674-2 (pbk.)
  1. Arlington National Cemetery (Arlington, Va.)--Juvenile literature. 2. Arlington (Va.)--Buildings, structures, etc.--Juvenile literature. I. Schaefer, Lola M., 1950- II. Title. III. Series.
  F234.A7S33 2005
  975.5'295--dc22
                            2005002034

Acknowledgments
The publishers would like to thank the following for permission to reproduce photographs:
Alamy p. 6 (Joe Sohm); Corbis p. 8; Empics/PA p. 27; Getty Images pp. 14–15 (Mark Wilson), 25 (Tim Sloan/AFP); Jill Birschbach/Harcourt Education Ltd pp. 4, 5, 7, 11, 12, 13, 16, 17, 18, 19, 20, 21, 22, 24, 25, 26, 27, 28, 29; Peter Newark's Americana Pictures pp. 9–10.

Cover photograph of Arlington National Cemetery reproduced with permission of Jill Birschbach/Harcourt Education Ltd.

In recognition of the National Park Service Rangers who are always present at the memorials, offering general information and interpretative tours. We thank you!

Some words are shown in bold, **like this**. You can find out what they mean by looking in the glossary.

Contents

Arlington National Cemetery

Arlington National Cemetery is across the Potomac River from Washington, D.C. Large trees shade graves on grassy hillsides. It is a quiet and peaceful place.

Arlington is the most famous U.S. cemetery.
It honors men and women who served their
country. More than 290,000 people are
buried there.

Those Brave Men and Women

Most graves at Arlington National Cemetery are for **veterans**. These are men and women who served in the U.S. **military**. A few have family members buried near them.

Some famous people are also buried at
Arlington. Here is the grave of Pierre
L'Enfant. His **monument** overlooks
Washington, D.C. – the city that he designed.

Arlington House

From 1831 to 1861, General and Mrs. Robert E. Lee owned a home called Arlington House. It was on the land that is now Arlington National Cemetery.

When the **Civil War** began, General Lee joined the **Confederate** Army. He and his wife moved to Richmond, Virginia. Arlington House was left empty.

A Burial Ground

Thousands of men died during the **Civil War**. Nearby cemeteries were full. President Lincoln ordered the army to find a new **burial** place.

Arlington became a **military** cemetery in 1864. **Union** and **Confederate** soldiers were buried there. Later some soldiers who had died in the earlier **Revolutionary War** were moved to this cemetery.

Most graves at Arlington National Cemetery are marked with simple **headstones**. Each stone shows the person's name, date of birth, and date of death.

Some **monuments** at the cemetery are large stones. Many have pictures and words on them. These **memorials** remind us of great people and events in American history.

Graveside Ceremony

Veterans are buried with a **military ceremony** at Arlington National Cemetery. An American flag covers the **casket** as it is brought to the graveside.

The **color guard** fires gunshots to honor the **veteran**. A **bugler** plays **taps**. The flag is folded and given to a family member.

Tomb of the Unknown Soldier

The Tomb of the Unknown Soldier is one of the most visited **memorials** at Arlington National Cemetery. Here lie the bodies of U.S. soldiers from different wars.

These soldiers' names are not known. This
memorial reminds us that they died for their
country. Guards protect the tomb day and
night as a symbol of respect and honor.

Civil War Memorials

Arlington National Cemetery has many reminders of the men who fought in the **Civil War**. This **memorial** honors 2,111 **Union** soldiers from that war.

Part of the **Confederate** Memorial in Arlington
shows the women of the South sending their
men off to fight. The graves of Confederate
soldiers are all around this **monument**.

U.S. Presidents

Two U.S. **presidents** are buried in Arlington National Cemetery. President William Howard Taft was buried there in 1930. President John F. Kennedy was laid to rest there in 1963.

An "eternal flame" marks the grave of
President Kennedy. This **memorial** is always
burning. It reminds a country of a president
who died while in office.

Remembering Sad Days

On February 15, 1898, the battleship *Maine* sank. The *Maine* **Memorial** honors the 264 men who died that day. The **mast** of the battleship is part of the memorial.

The *Challenger* Memorial reminds us that on January 28, 1986, the space shuttle *Challenger* exploded. The seven people on board that day all lost their lives.

Memorial Amphitheater

The **Memorial** Amphitheater is near the center of Arlington. It is a large, round building without a roof. Rows of seats face a stage.

Ceremonies for **Memorial Day** and **Veterans Day** are held here each year. Many people take part to honor the **veterans** who gave their lives in American wars.

25

Visiting Arlington National Cemetery

Arlington National Cemetery is larger than 600 football fields. When you visit stop in the cemetery office. Ask for a map and directions to the graves and **memorials**.

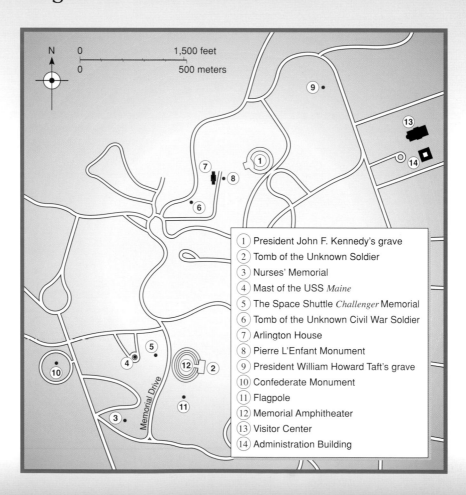

N   0   1,500 feet

0   500 meters

Memorial Drive

1. President John F. Kennedy's grave
2. Tomb of the Unknown Soldier
3. Nurses' Memorial
4. Mast of the USS *Maine*
5. The Space Shuttle *Challenger* Memorial
6. Tomb of the Unknown Civil War Soldier
7. Arlington House
8. Pierre L'Enfant Monument
9. President William Howard Taft's grave
10. Confederate Monument
11. Flagpole
12. Memorial Amphitheater
13. Visitor Center
14. Administration Building

Signs and section markers will help guide you across the cemetery. Look at all the **headstones**. Think about these brave soldiers who fought for **freedom**.

Fact File

Arlington National Cemetery

★ The oldest grave at Arlington belongs to Mary Randolph. She was Mrs. Robert E. Lee's godmother. She was buried on the grounds in 1828, long before Arlington was a cemetery.

★ In 1864 the first **military burial** at Arlington National Cemetery was of Private William Christman.

★ John Lincoln Clem was the youngest soldier in the **Civil War**. He was only nine years old! His grave is in Arlington National Cemetery.

★ All standard **headstones** in Arlington National Cemetery are paid for and put up by the United States government.

★ During the summer mowers cut the grass in Arlington National Cemetery every day. This costs the cemetery $1.2 million a year.

Timeline

Arlington National Cemetery

- ★ 1831–1861   Mr. and Mrs. Robert E. Lee live in Arlington House
- ★ 1861–1864   **Union** soldiers use Arlington House as one of their headquarters
- ★ 1864   Arlington becomes a national cemetery
- ★ 1866   2,111 unknown Civil War soldiers are buried in Arlington
- ★ 1913   The *Maine* **Memorial** is **dedicated**
- ★ 1914   The **Confederate** Memorial is dedicated
- ★ 1920   Memorial Amphitheater is finished
- ★ 1921   Tomb of the Unknown Soldier is set up
- ★ 1986   The *Challenger* Memorial is dedicated

Glossary

bugler person who plays an instrument similar to a trumpet, but without keys; bugle sounds often send signals to soldiers

burial placing of a dead body in the earth

casket long box in which a dead person is placed before burial

ceremony special event to mark something important

Civil War U.S. war of 1861 to 1865, in which northern states fought against southern states

color guard guard of honor for the colors of an organization, such as the military forces

Confederate of or about the Confederate States of America, the group of southern states that fought against the Union soldiers in the Civil War

dedicate have a ceremony that opens a new bridge, hospital, or memorial

freedom having the right to say, behave, or move around as you please

headstone marker that is put at the head of a grave. It usually gives the name, date of birth, and date of death of the person buried there.

mast tall pole on the deck of a boat or ship that holds up its sails

memorial something that is built to help people remember a person or an event

Memorial Day holiday celebrated in the United States on the last Monday of May to honor Americans who have died in wars

military to do with soldiers, the armed forces, or war

monument statue or building that reminds people of an even or a person

president person chosen by the people of a republic to be their leader

Revolutionary War war of 1775 to 1783 in which the United States fought for freedom from British rule

taps simple tune usually played by a bugler at a military burial

Union of or about the United States, or the northern states, during the Civil War

veteran someone who has served in the armed forces

Veterans Day November 11, a day honoring men and women who served in the armed forces and fought in wars for the United States

More Books to Read

An older reader can help you with these books:

Ansary, Mir Tamim. *Memorial Day*. Des Plaines, Ill.: Heinemann Library, 1998.

Ansary, Mir Tamim. *Veterans Day*. Des Plaines, Ill.: Heinemann Library, 1998.

Temple, Bob. *Arlington National Cemetery: Where Heroes Rest.* Chanhassen, Minn.: Child's World, 2001.

Visiting Arlington National Cemetery

Arlington National Cemetery is open 8:00 A.M. to 7:00 P.M. from April 1 to September 30. It is open 8:00 A.M. to 5:00 P.M. from October 1 to March 31. You do not have to pay to visit Arlington National Cemetery.

You can go on a shuttle tour if you buy a ticket at the Visitor Center. Shuttle tours run every day except Christmas (December 25). Shuttle tour hours are: April to August: 8:30 A.M. to 6:30 P.M. and September to March 9:30 A.M. to 4:30 P.M.

To ask for a brochure and map of Arlington National Cemetery, write to this address:

Arlington National Cemetery
Public Affairs Office
103 Third Ave.
Ft. McNair, D.C. 20319.

Index